I Belong to the Muslim Faith

Katie Dicker and Zohal Azizi

WAYLAND

Published in paperback in 2014 by Wayland

Wayland
Hachette Children's Books
338 Euston Road
London NW1 3BH

Wayland Australia
Level 17/207 Kent Street
Sydney, NSW 2000

Managing Editor: Rasha Elsaeed

Produced for Wayland by

White-Thomson Publishing Ltd.
www.wtpub.co.uk
+44 (0)843 208 7460

Editor: Katie Dicker
Designer: Clare Nicholas
Editorial consultant: Daniel Owers
Photographer: Chris Fairclough

British Library Cataloguing in Publication Data
Dicker, Katie
   I belong to the Muslim faith
   1. Islam - Juvenile literature
   I. Title II. Azizi, Zohal
   297

ISBN 978 0 7502 8429 5

Printed in China

Wayland is a division of Hachette Children's Books,
an Hachette UK company.
www.hachette.co.uk

Acknowledgements

The author and publisher would like to thank the
following people for their help and participation in
this book:
The Azizi family, Bindu Rai, Mohammad Hoda and
all at the Central Mosque, Wembley.

The website addresses (URLs) included in this book
were valid at the time of going to press. However,
because of the nature of the Internet, it is possible
that some addresses may have changed, or sites may
have changed or closed down since publication. While
the author and publisher regret any inconvenience
this may cause the readers, no responsibility for any
such changes can be accepted by either the author
or the publisher.

Disclaimer

The text in this book is based on the experience of
one family. While every effort has been made to offer
accurate and clearly expressed information, the author
and publisher acknowledge that some explanations
may not be relevant to those who practise their faith
in a different way.

10 9 8 7 6 5 4 3 2

Contents

A celebration

Hi, I'm Zohal. Today it's **Eid-ul-Fitr** and my family are celebrating the end of **Ramadan**. We're Muslims – we follow the religion of Islam. Last night, there was a new moon which meant that Eid-ul-Fitr could begin.

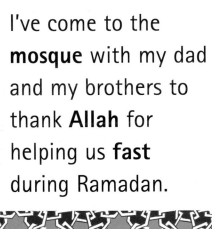

I've come to the **mosque** with my dad and my brothers to thank **Allah** for helping us **fast** during Ramadan.

The mosque is really busy today. Everyone is gathering outside before we go in to **pray**. Tents have been put up beside the mosque so there is space for everyone.

This man is giving money to help the poor. We share the things that Allah has given us, especially during Ramadan.

At the mosque

We can go to the mosque every day, but Friday is a special day for Muslims. Just after midday, men gather at the mosque to say the Friday prayer called Jumu'ah.

The mosque is a short drive from our house. It has two prayer halls and smaller rooms where we can meet with our friends.

We go to the mosque to **worship** Allah with other Muslims. Allah created the world and looks after us. It makes me happy to think of all the good things that Allah has given me.

We take off our shoes before we go into the mosque because we want to keep it clean. It's also to show our respect for Allah.

Salat

Muslims pray five times a day – at dawn, midday, in the afternoon, at sunset and just before bed. These prayers are called Salat. We say our prayers at home or at the mosque.

Men and women worship in different halls at the mosque. But wherever we pray, we all face towards **Mecca**.

The prayer halls are very large. There are no pictures or statues that might distract us – we only think about Allah when we pray. We praise Allah our creator, and ask for his help in our lives.

These clocks show the times of Salat and the Friday prayer. The times change each day, depending on the position of the sun.

How do we pray?

There are four main positions of prayer. We stand up so that Allah can hear what we are saying, then we kneel and bow to show our respect. Finally we touch our hands and our head to the ground.

We pray in a language called Arabic. During our prayers we say 'Allaho-Akbar' which means 'Allah is great'.

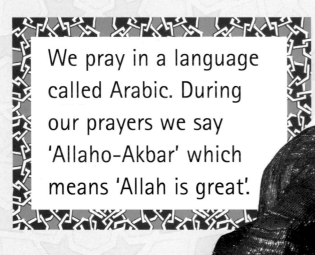

Before we pray, we wash our hands and our face. It's important to be clean and pure in what we say and do, whenever we worship Allah. We use prayer mats so we don't have to touch the floor.

We all face towards Mecca when we pray at home, just like we do at the mosque.

Who was Muhammad?

Muhammad (peace be upon him) was a **prophet**. He was born in Mecca nearly 1,500 years ago. Every time we mention his name we say 'peace be upon him (pbuh)' to show our respect for him.

The **imam** leads the prayers at the mosque. He shows us how to follow the Islamic way of life, as the prophets did long ago.

The prophets taught people about the wonders of Allah and passed on his wisdom. Allah's teachings are written in our holy book, the **Qu'ran**. His words were given to Muhammad (pbuh) by the angel Gabriel, Allah's messenger.

The Qu'ran is full of beautiful rhyming verses. When I read the Qu'ran, I put it on a wooden stand to keep it safe and clean.

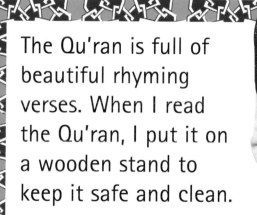

My guide to life

The Qu'ran is written in Arabic. Dad helps me to understand what the words mean. The Qu'ran teaches us how important it is to obey Allah. Allah's words also remind me of the power of goodness over evil.

When I'm unsure of something, I turn to the Qu'ran to guide me. It's comforting to hear Allah's words.

I wear a scarf called a Hijab each day as a sign of **modesty**. I also follow sayings called Hadith. These words describe the way Muhammad (pbuh) followed Allah's teachings in his life.

I keep my head and shoulders covered as the Qu'ran teaches me. On festival days, I also like to put these henna decorations on my hands.

Helping others

Allah has sent angels to watch over and record my deeds. One day, Allah will choose whether I go to **heaven** when I die. I try to have good manners and to behave as Allah has taught me.

I often help Dad with the shopping – it's good to lend a hand. We've been to this shop to buy halal meat.

At school, I was asked to be a counsellor. People in my class come to see me if they're worried about something. I'm good at listening and I try to make them feel better.

Allah teaches us to be kind and thoughtful to others. I try to follow Allah's guidance every day.

Food and fasting

The Qu'ran says we shouldn't eat or drink when it's daylight during the month of Ramadan. Being hungry and thirsty teaches us to control our feelings and to be grateful for what we have.

During Ramadan, we think of other people who do not have enough to eat. Our dinner tastes very good when we've been fasting!

The Qu'ran also says we're not allowed to eat some foods. We don't eat pork or any animals that eat meat, or have not been slaughtered in the name of Allah. This is because the Qu'ran says they're unclean.

We describe foods as halal or haram. We can eat halal food, but the Qu'ran says haram food is unlawful.

Muslim festivals

At Eid-ul-Fitr, we celebrate the end of the fast that we have all shared together. Over this three-day festival, lots of friends and family will visit us.

On festival days, we have a special meal and share sweet foods to bring everyone a sweet time ahead.

At **Eid-ul-Adha** we think about how we should obey Allah's teachings. We remember that the prophet Abraham (pbuh) was willing to sacrifice his son for Allah. This festival comes at the end of the **Hajj**.

I wear this dress to make me feel special on festival days. Some of the threads are made from real silver!

Glossary and further information

Allah – an Arabic name for God.

fast – to go without food.

Hajj – a special journey when Muslims try to visit Mecca as a sign of respect to Allah.

heaven – the place where Muslims believe they will go to live when they die.

imam – a person who leads Muslim worship.

Mecca – a place in Saudi Arabia where the prophet Muhammad was born.

modesty – to dress in a way that does not show off parts of the body.

mosque – a building where Muslims go to worship Allah.

pray – to talk to God. Muslims pray to Allah to give thanks, or to ask for help or forgiveness.

prophet – a messenger sent by God.

Qu'ran – a special book full of Allah's words.

Ramadan – A month of fasting during daylight hours.

worship – to show love and respect to Allah.

Did you know?

- Islam began in Saudi Arabia almost 1,500 years ago.
- The word Islam means 'peace'.
- There are over one thousand million Muslims today, mostly living in the Middle East, Asia and North Africa.
- There are two main groups in the Muslim religion, called Sunnis and Shiites.
- The dates of Muslim festivals follow a lunar calendar.

Activities

1. Arrange to visit a local mosque. Write down all the things you can see. Which way is the direction of Mecca?
2. Find the location of Mecca on a map. Research using books or the internet to find out why Mecca is so important to Muslims.
3. Draw a design for a prayer mat using Muslim symbols.

Books to read

- *Islam for Children* by Ahmad Von Denffer, Islamic Foundation, 2007
- *Islamic Stories (Storyteller)* by Anita Ganeri, Evans Brothers, 2006

Websites

http://atschool.eduweb.co.uk/carolrb/islam/islamintro.html

A basic introduction to Islam for primary school children, with clear text and colourful photographs and illustrations.

http://www.hitchams.suffolk.sch.uk/mosque/default.htm

This website introduces children to life at a mosque and daily life as a Muslim, with simple text and colour photographs.

Organisations

The Muslim Association of Britain
124 Harrowdene Road
Wembley
Middlesex
HA0 2JF

Muslim festivals

Al Hijra (December / January)
The Islamic New Year.

Mawlid (February / March)
The birthday of the prophet Muhammad.

Eid-ul-Fitr (October)
A three-day festival to end the fast of Ramadan.

Eid-ul-Adha (December / January)
A three-day festival when Muslims remember that the prophet Abraham was willing to sacrifice his son for Allah.

Muslim symbols

Star and crescent – the Moon and star are used as a symbol of the way that Islam guides and lights a Muslim's way through life.

Arabic script – some Arabic words are used as a symbol of Islam. The word for 'Allah' for example, is often used as a decoration in Muslim books and pictures.

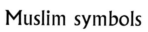

Index